SUSAN AND JAMES PATTERSON

Illustrated by
HSINPING PAN

BIG WORDS for little geniuses

JIMMY Patterson Books
Little, Brown and Company
New York Boston London

Arachibutyrophobia
(Ah-RACK-ee-byoo-tee-ro-FO-bee-ya)

Arachibutyrophobia is the **alarming** fear of peanut butter sticking to the top of your mouth!

Bibliomania (bib-lee-oh-MAY-nee-ah)

You have **bibliomania** if you love to collect as many **books** as you can.

Catawampus (ca-tah-WOMP-us)

Catawampus means tilted, diagonal, or just a little bit **crooked**.

Dulcifluous (dull-SIH-floo-iss)

The **delightful** word **dulcifluous** sounds like what it means: flowing sweetly and gently.

Empyreal (em-pie-REE-ul)

Empyreal means heavenly, like the **enchanting** blue color of the sky on a sunny day.

Flibbertigibbet *(flih-ber-tee-JIH-bit)*

A **friend** who loves to talk and talk can be called a **flibbertigibbet.**

Gobbledygook (GAH-bul-dee-gook)

If you hear words that sound a little **goofy** or nonsensical, you're listening to **gobbledygook**!

G WHACK A

Doodle doooooo

SHOOKA WOOKA LOOKA

MUMSY LAY

HARGA PARGA

LUMSY oogly

Gobbeldy...

googly

FARF...mie

BAR

TARSH

BOOMiE

LOOMiE

KARZOOMiE

MAIA CHANCA!

Horripilation (haw-rih-puh-LAY-shun)

If you're cold, scared, or excited, you may get **horripilation**, or goose bumps, on your **head** or body.

Idioglossia (ih-dee-oh-GLOH-see-ya)

If you share a secret language with a friend, it's called an **idioglossia**.

Juxtaposition (jucks-ta-poe-ZIH-shun)

When you put things side by side, you've **just** made a **juxtaposition**!

Kerfuffle (kerr-FUH-ful)

Have you ever **kicked** up a big fuss about something, like baking a cake? That's called a **kerfuffle**!

Lilliputian (li-lee-PYOO-shun)

Lilliputian means very tiny or **little**, especially when describing a person.

Magnanimous (mag-NA-nih-mus)

If you're **magnanimous**, you like to share your **most** favorite toys with your friends.

Nincompoop (NIN-come-poop)

When you're acting a little silly or **naughty**, you may be called a **nincompoop**!

Onomatopoeia (AH-noh-ma-toe-PEE-ya)

An **onomatopoeia** is a sound word, like moo, splat, and **oink**!
Can you think of any others?

OINK

BAA

WHOO

SPROing

CLICK CLACK

ROAR

Pulchritudinous (puhl-kri-TOO-dih-nus)

Pretty and **pulchritudinous** mean the same thing, but one is much more fun to say!

Quokka (KWOH-ka)

The **quokka** is called the happiest animal in the world because it smiles **quite** a lot!

Rapscallion (rap-SKALL-yen)

A **rapscallion** is someone who **really** likes to cause trouble.

S

Stelliferous *(stell-IH-fur-us)*

When the night sky is filled with **stars**, it's a **stelliferous sight**!

Tokus *(TOOK-us)*

Your **tokus** has lots of funny-sounding names, like heinie, **tush**, and bum-bum!

Undulating (UN-dyoo-lay-ting)

Something that moves **up** and down is **undulating**, like the waves of the ocean.

Volitant (VOLL-ih-tint)

It would feel **very** exciting to be **volitant** and fly through the air like a bird.

Whirligig (WHIR-lee-gig)

A **whirligig** spins around and around, like a pinwheel in the **wind**.

Xanthochroism (zan-THOCK-ro-ih-zim)

Animals that have **xanthochroism** are bright yellow or orange, like goldfish.

Yaffingale (YAH-fin-gale)

A **yaffingale** is a colorful bird with **yellow** and green feathers on its body and red on top of its head.

Zamboni *(zam-BO-nee)*

Zamboni is the name of the big machine that **zooms** around an ice rink to smooth out the ice.

Here are more BIG WORDS for you to learn.

Adamantine *(a-dah-MAN-teen)* — unbreakable

Bumfuzzle *(BUM-fuzz-ul)* — to confuse someone

Collywobbles *(CALL-ee-woh-bulls)* — a tummyache

Discombobulate *(dis-come-BOB-yoo-late)* — to confuse someone

Erinaceous *(air-in-AY-shuss)* — having to do with or looking like a hedgehog

Felicitations *(feh-liss-ih-TAY-shuns)* — kind words to make people feel happy

Grandiloquence *(gran-DIH-loh-kwens)* — using big words or lots of style

Humongous *(hyoo-MUN-gus)* — very, very large

Isthmus *(ISS-muss)* — a thin strip of land that connects two bigger areas of land

Jillion *(JILL-yun)* — a very high number

Kumquat *(COME-kwat)* — a sweet orange-colored fruit

Loquacious *(low-KWAY-shuss)* — very talkative

Moppet *(MOH-pet)* — a young child

Nephelococcygia *(NEH-fell-oh-kok-SIH-jee-uh)* — finding familiar shapes in clouds

Which is the most fun word to say?

Ozostomia *(oh-zo-STO-mee-ya)* — bad-smelling breath

Pandiculation *(pan-dik-yoo-LAY-shun)* — stretching and yawning at the same time

Quixotic *(kwik-SAW-tick)* — when you think that your dreams can come true

Rigmarole *(RIG-ma-roll)* — something that is complicated and takes a long time

Syzygy *(SIH-zih-jee)* — when objects are lined up, especially the sun, the moon, and the earth

Tarradiddle *(tare-ah-DIH-dul)* — a small fib

Uxorious *(ucks-OH-ree-us)* — very much in love with one's wife

Vichyssoise *(vih-shee-SWAHZ)* — a creamy soup made with potatoes and onions

Whangdoodle *(WANG-doo-dull)* — an imaginary creature from children's books

Xylophone *(ZY-lo-fone)* — a musical instrument played by hitting wooden bars

Yarnwindle *(YARN-win-dill)* — a tool for winding yarn into a ball

Zoosemiotics *(zoe-ah-seh-mee-AW-ticks)* — the study of how animals communicate, like birds singing and dogs wagging their tails

For Lorraine: A numerologist and a cruciverbalist in the most frabjous sort of way! — S. P.

For Jack: A woolgathering whangdoodle if ever there was one! — J. P.

For Ray: The incomparable life companion who is perpetually there for me! — H. P.

ABOUT THIS BOOK

This book was edited by Jenny Bak and designed by Gail Doobinin with art direction by Tracy Shaw. The production was supervised by Lisa Ferris, and the production editor was Betsy Uhrig.
The text was set in Bernhard Gothic and illustrations were created using Adobe Illustrator and Photoshop.

JIMMY Patterson Books / Little, Brown and Company / Hachette Book Group / 1290 Avenue of the Americas, New York, NY 10104 / JimmyPatterson.org
First Edition: September 2017
JIMMY Patterson Books is an imprint of Little, Brown and Company, a division of Hachette Book Group, Inc. The Little, Brown name and logo are trademarks of Hachette Book Group, Inc.
The JIMMY Patterson name and logo are trademarks of JBP Business, LLC.
Zamboni is a registered trademark of Frank J. Zamboni & Co., Inc.
The publisher is not responsible for websites (or their content) that are not owned by the publisher.
The Hachette Speakers Bureau provides a wide range of authors for speaking events. To find out more, go to hachettespeakersbureau.com or call (866) 376-6591.
ISBN 978-0-316-50293-1 / LCCN 2017938654
10 9 8 7 6 5 4 3 2 1
IM / Printed in China